Johann Sebastian BACH

(1685 – 1750)

Sonata for Flute and Basso continuo, BWV 1033
C Major / Ut majeur / C-Dur

Edited by
Evelin Degen

DOWANI International

Preface

This volume introduces you to Johann Sebastian Bach's Sonata in C Major for flute and basso continuo (BWV 1033). It is a four-movement piece in the style of an Italian "Sonata da camera". Our edition has been completely revised and given a new *DOWANI 3 Tempi Play Along* recording with harpsichord accompaniment at all speeds, along with a new musical text containing the solo part and a piano reduction.

The CD opens with the concert version of each movement. After tuning your instrument (Track 1), you can begin to work. Your first practice session should be at the slow tempo. If your stereo system is equipped with a balance control, you can place either the flute part or the harpsichord accompaniment in the foreground by adjusting the control. The flute will always remain softly audible in the background as a guide. In the middle position, both instruments can be heard at the same volume. If you do not have a balance control, you can listen to the solo flute on one loudspeaker and the harpsichord on the other. Having mastered the piece at slow tempo, you can now advance to the medium and original tempos. The harpsichord accompaniment can be heard on both channels (without flute) in stereo quality. All of the versions were recorded live. The names of the musicians are listed on the last page of this volume; further information can be found in the Internet at www.dowani.com.

In keeping with its style, this music relies heavily on elements of improvisation, and we have included only the most essential embellishments and phrase marks. Players are invited to add trills, mordents, slurs and so forth at their own discretion. The same holds true, of course, for the realization of the figured bass (basso continuo or harpsichord), as can clearly be heard on the recording.

We wish you lots of fun playing from our *DOWANI 3 Tempi Play Along* editions and hope that your musicality and diligence will enable you to play the concert version as soon as possible. Our goal is to give you the essential conditions you need for effective practicing through motivation, enjoyment and fun.

Your DOWANI Team

Avant-propos

Notre édition vous présente la sonate pour flûte et basse continue BWV 1033 en Ut majeur de Johann Sebastian Bach. Cette sonate est divisée en quatre mouvements dans le style italien de la "Sonata da camera". Il s'agit d'une édition complètement révisée : nouvel enregistrement *DOWANI 3 Tempi Play Along* avec accompagnement de clavecin dans tous les différents tempos ainsi qu'une nouvelle partition, comprenant partie soliste et réduction pour piano.

Le CD vous permettra d'entendre d'abord la version de concert de chaque mouvement. Après avoir accordé votre instrument (plage n° 1), vous pourrez commencer le travail musical. Le premier contact avec le morceau devrait se faire à un tempo lent. Si votre chaîne hi-fi dispose d'un réglage de balance, vous pouvez l'utiliser pour mettre au premier plan soit la flûte, soit l'accompagnement au clavecin. La flûte restera cependant toujours audible très doucement à l'arrière-plan. En équilibrant la balance, vous entendrez les deux instruments à volume égal. Si vous ne disposez pas de réglage de balance, vous entendrez l'instrument soliste sur un des haut-parleurs et le clavecin sur l'autre. Après avoir étudié le morceau à un tempo lent, vous pourrez ensuite travailler à un tempo modéré et au tempo original. Dans ces deux tempos, vous entendrez l'accompagnement de clavecin sur les deux canaux en stéréo (sans la partie de flûte). Toutes les versions ont été enregistrées en direct. Vous trouverez les noms des artistes qui ont participé aux enregistrements sur la dernière page de cette édition ; pour obtenir plus de renseignements, veuillez consulter notre site Internet : www.dowani.com.

Cette musique repose à l'origine beaucoup sur des éléments d'improvisation ; c'est pourquoi nous n'avons noté que très peu d'ornements et de phrasés. Chaque musicien peut ou doit ajouter ses propres indications (trilles, mordants, liaisons etc.). Cela concerne également la réalisation de la basse chiffrée (basse continue ou clavecin) – comme on l'entend bien sur notre enregistrement.

Nous vous souhaitons beaucoup de plaisir à faire de la musique avec la collection *DOWANI 3 Tempi Play Along* et nous espérons que votre musicalité et votre application vous amèneront aussi rapidement que possible à la version de concert. Notre but est de vous offrir les bases nécessaires pour un travail efficace par la motivation et le plaisir.

Les Éditions DOWANI

Vorwort

Mit dieser Ausgabe präsentieren wir Ihnen Johann Sebastian Bachs Sonate für Flöte und Basso continuo BWV 1033 in C-Dur. Es handelt sich um eine viersätzige Sonate im Stil der italienischen „Sonata da camera". Diese Ausgabe ist eine komplett revidierte Neuausgabe mit einer neuen *DOWANI 3 Tempi Play Along*-Aufnahme mit Cembalo-Begleitung in allen Tempi sowie einer neuen Notenausgabe mit Solostimme und Klavierauszug.

Auf der CD können Sie zuerst die Konzertversion eines jeden Satzes anhören. Nach dem Stimmen Ihres Instrumentes (Track 1) kann die musikalische Arbeit beginnen. Ihr erster Übe-Kontakt mit dem Stück sollte im langsamen Tempo stattfinden. Wenn Ihre Stereoanlage über einen Balance-Regler verfügt, können Sie durch Drehen des Reglers entweder die Flöte oder die Cembalobegleitung stufenlos in den Vordergrund blenden. Die Flöte bleibt jedoch immer – wenn auch sehr leise – hörbar. In der Mittelposition erklingen beide Instrumente gleich laut. Falls Sie keinen Balance-Regler haben, hören Sie das Soloinstrument auf dem einen Lautsprecher, das Cembalo auf dem anderen. Nachdem Sie das Stück im langsamen Tempo einstudiert haben, können Sie danach im mittelschnellen und

originalen Tempo musizieren. Die Cembalo-Begleitung erklingt hierbei auf beiden Kanälen (ohne Flöte) in Stereo-Qualität. Alle eingespielten Versionen wurden live aufgenommen. Die Namen der Künstler finden Sie auf der letzten Seite dieser Ausgabe; ausführlichere Informationen können Sie im Internet unter www.dowani.com nachlesen.

Da diese Musik ihrem Ursprung entsprechend sehr stark auf improvisatorischen Elementen beruht, wurden nur die nötigsten Verzierungen und Phrasierungen notiert. Der Spieler oder die Spielerin darf/soll gerne eigene Ergänzungen (Triller, Mordente, Bindungen usw.) hinzufügen. Dies gilt natürlich auch für die Ausführung des Generalbasses (Basso continuo oder Cembalo) – wie in der Aufnahme deutlich zu hören ist.

Wir wünschen Ihnen viel Spaß beim Musizieren mit unseren *DOWANI 3 Tempi Play Along*-Ausgaben und hoffen, dass Ihre Musikalität und Ihr Fleiß Sie möglichst bald bis zur Konzertversion führen werden. Unser Ziel ist es, Ihnen durch Motivation, Freude und Spaß die notwendigen Voraussetzungen für effektives Üben zu schaffen.

Ihr DOWANI Team

Sonata

for Flute and Basso continuo, BWV 1033
C Major / Ut majeur / C-Dur

J. S. Bach (1685 – 1750)
Continuo Realization: G. Stöver

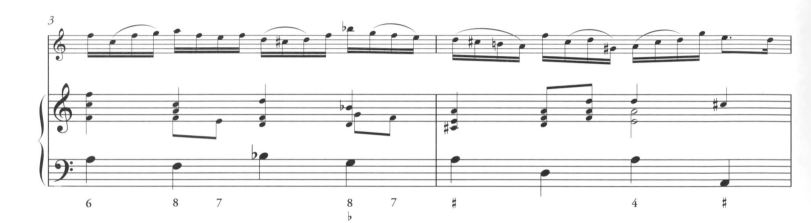

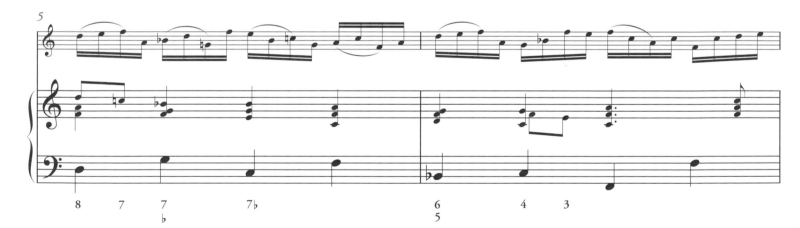

DOW 5507

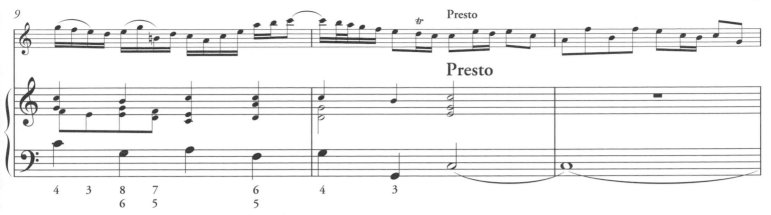

Presto

6

Flute

Sonata

for Flute and Basso continuo, BWV 1033
C Major / Ut majeur / C-Dur

J. S. Bach (1685 – 1750)
Edited by E. Degen

DOW 5507

2

Allegro

4

8

11

15

18

21

24

27

10 | 18 | 26

III ④

Adagio

IV ⑤

Menuett I

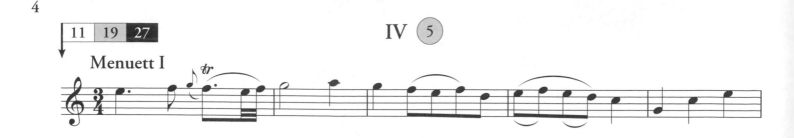

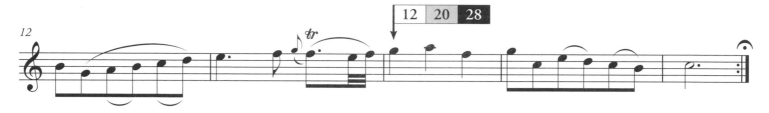

V

Menuett II

Menuett I ab initio

Johann Sebastian BACH

(1685 – 1750)

Sonata for Flute and Basso continuo, BWV 1033
C Major / Ut majeur / C-Dur

Basso continuo / Basse continue / Generalbass

DOWANI International

Sonata

for Flute and Basso continuo, BWV 1033
C Major / Ut majeur / C-Dur

J. S. Bach (1685 – 1750)

I

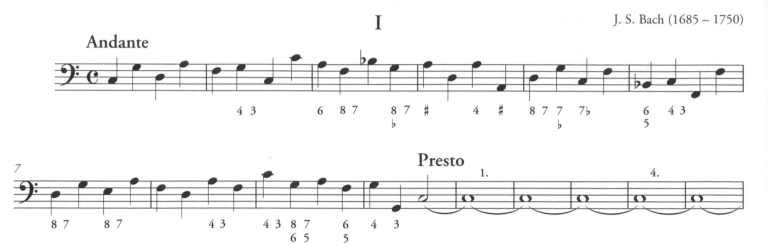

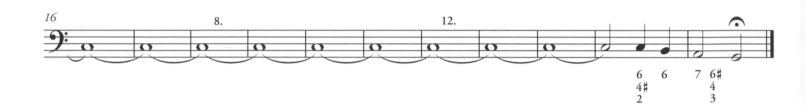

II

DOW 5507

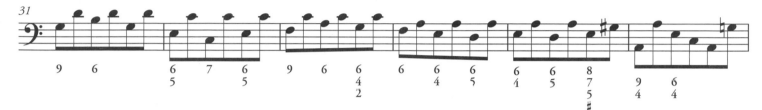

III

Adagio

IV

Menuett I

V

Menuett II

Menuett I ab initio

SUITE FOR STRINGS

Robert Washburn

I LITTLE MARCH

Printed in the U.S.A.

OXFORD UNIVERSITY PRESS

II   SONG

III   SCHERZO

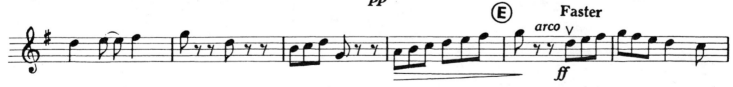

VIOLIN I

IV FINALE

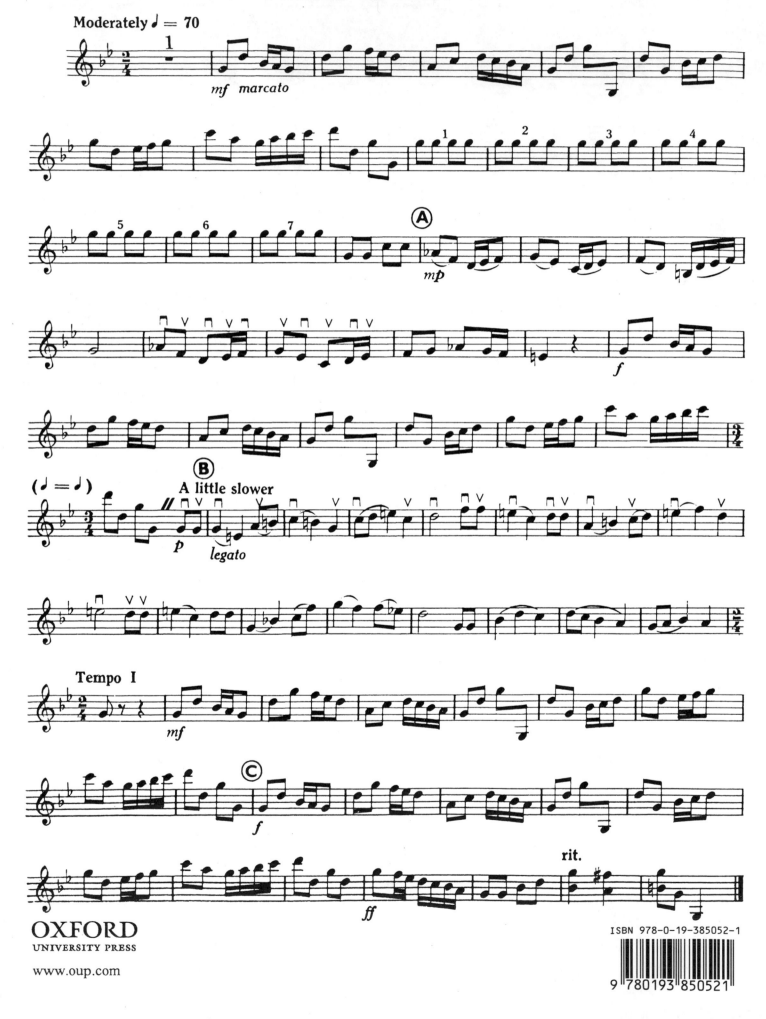

OXFORD

UNIVERSITY PRESS

www.oup.com

ISBN 978-0-19-385052-1

9 780193 850521

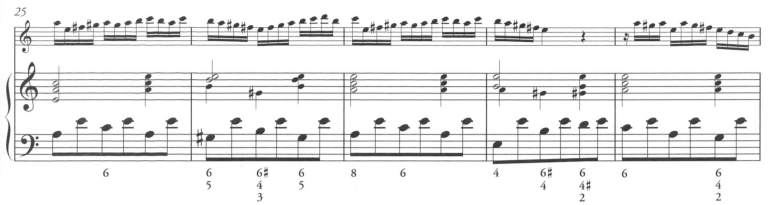

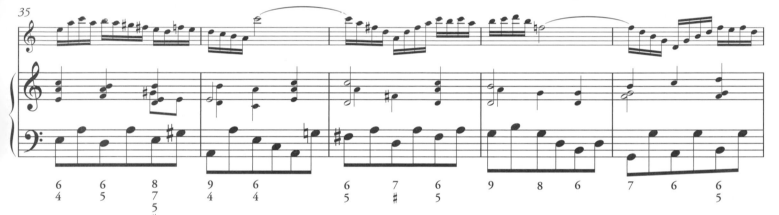

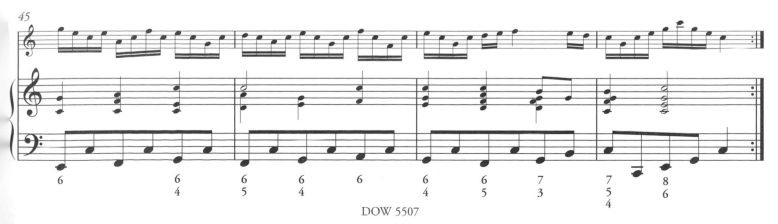

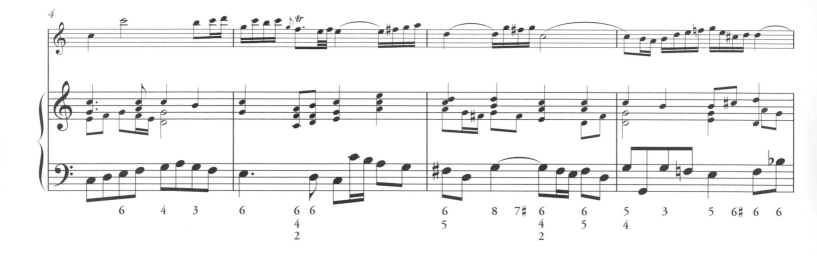

Menuett I

Menuett I

Menuett II

Menuett I ab initio

ENGLISH

DOWANI CD:

- Track No. 1   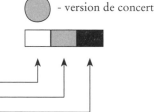   - tuning notes

- Track numbers in circles   ⬤   - concert version

- Track numbers in squares

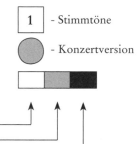

   - slow Play Along Tempo
   - intermediate Play Along Tempo
   - original Play Along Tempo

- Additional tracks for longer movements or pieces

- **Concert version:** flute and harpsichord

- **Slow tempo:** The flute can be faded in or out by means of the balance control. Channel 1: flute solo; channel 2: harpsichord accompaniment with flute in the background; middle position: both channels at the same volume

- **Intermediate tempo:** harpsichord only

- **Original tempo:** harpsichord only

Please note that the recorded version of the harpsichord accompaniment ma[y] differ slightly from the sheet music. This is due to the spontaneous characte[r] of live music making and the artistic freedom of the musicians. The original sheet music for the solo part is, of course, not affected.

FRANÇAIS

DOWANI CD :

- Plage N° 1   1   - diapason

- N° de plage dans un cercle   ⬤   - version de concert

- N° de plage dans un rectangle

   - tempo lent play along
   - tempo moyen play along
   - tempo original play along

- Plages supplémentaires pour mouvements ou morceaux longs

- **Version de concert :** flûte et clavecin

- **Tempo lent :** Vous pouvez choisir – en réglant la balance du lecteur CD – entre les versions avec ou sans flûte. 1er canal : flûte ; 2nd canal : accompagnement de clavecin avec flûte en fond sonore ; au milieu : les deux canaux au même volume

- **Tempo moyen :** seulement l'accompagnement de clavecin

- **Tempo original :** seulement l'accompagnement de clavecin

L'enregistrement de l'accompagnement de clavecin peut présenter quelques différences mineures par rapport au texte de la partition. Ceci est du à la liberté artistique des musiciens et résulte d'un jeu spontané et vivant, mais n'affecte, bien entendu, d'aucune manière la partie soliste.

DEUTSCH

DOWANI CD:

- Track Nr. 1   1   - Stimmtöne

- Trackangabe im Kreis   ⬤   - Konzertversion

- Trackangabe im Rechteck

   - langsames Play Along Tempo
   - mittleres Play Along Tempo
   - originales Play Along Tempo

- Zusätzliche Tracks bei längeren Sätzen oder Stücken

- **Konzertversion:** Flöte und Cembalo

- **Langsames Tempo:** Flöte kann mittels Balance-Regler ein- und ausgeblendet werden. 1. Kanal: Flöte solo; 2. Kanal: Cembalobegleitung mit Flöte im Hintergrund; Mitte: beide Kanäle in gleicher Lautstärke

- **Mittleres Tempo:** nur Cembalo

- **Originaltempo:** nur Cembalo

Die Cembalobegleitung auf der CD-Aufnahme kann gegenüber dem Notentext kleine Abweichungen aufweisen. Dies geht in der Regel auf die künstlerische Freiheit der Musiker und auf spontanes, lebendiges Musizier[en] zurück. Die Solostimme bleibt davon selbstverständlich unangetastet.

DOWANI - 3 Tempi Play Along is published by:
DOWANI International Est.
Industriestrasse 24 / Postfach 156, FL-9487 Bendern,
Principality of Liechtenstein
Phone: ++423 370 11 15, Fax ++423 370 19 44
Email: info@dowani.com
www.dowani.com

Recording & Digital Mastering: Peter Böving, Germany
CD-Production: MediaMotion, The Netherlands
Music Notation: Notensatz Thomas Metzinger, Germany
Design: Andreas Haselwanter, Austria
Printed by: Zrinski d.d., Croatia
Made in the Principality of Liechtenstein

Concert Versi[on]
Evelin Degen, Flu[te]
Sigrun Stephan, Harpsicho[rd]

3 Tempi Accompanime[nt]
Slo[w]
Sigrun Stephan, Harpsicho[rd]

Intermedia[te]
Sigrun Stephan, Harpsicho[rd]

Origin[al]
Sigrun Stephan, Harpsicho[rd]